LONG STORY SHORT

LONG STORY SHORT

MJ Bartholomew

Copyright © 2013 by MJ Bartholomew.

Library of Congress Control Number:		2013908224
ISBN:	Hardcover	978-1-4836-3760-0
	Softcover	978-1-4836-3759-4
	Ebook	978-1-4836-3761-7

All rights reserved. No part of this book may be reproduced or transmitted in any form or by any means, electronic or mechanical, including photocopying, recording, or by any information storage and retrieval system, without permission in writing from the copyright owner.

This book was printed in the United States of America.

Follow MJ Bartholomew on Facebook.

Rev. date: 06/22/2013

To order additional copies of this book, contact:
Xlibris Corporation
1-888-795-4274
www.Xlibris.com
Orders@Xlibris.com
131099

Contents

Acknowledgment 7
Karma 11
Truth Is a Slippery Slope 12
Memory 13
Look at Me 14
Words Without Thought 15
Dancing with Madness 16
Elevator Chatter 17
I Am Unable 18
Somewhere in Between 19
The Givers The Takers 20
A Woman of Subtle Distinction 21
Miss Manners 22
Chanel, Gucci, Louis Vuitton, Juicy Couture, Burberry, Balenciaga 23
Opportunist 24
Black and Blue 25
Oreo 26
Could Have Been 28
Left Behind 29
Late Sunday Afternoon 30
To the Abyss 31
I 32
Best Friends 33
The Wife Her Husband His Mistress 34
She 36
Unhinged 37
god 38
When 39
Achilles' Heel 40
An Evening to Play at Seduction 41
Emotional Affair 42

Six Feet Deep 43
Dreaming 44
Taken 45
Forgotten Memories 46
So What 47
The Green Dress 48
Kaleidoscope of Memories 50
Widowed 52
Hardness of Heart 53
Me and My Pop 54
Child of Mine 55
A Mother's Love 56
The One 57
Beautiful Boy 58
Sons 60
Lost and Found 61
Delinquent 62
The Family 65
Believe 66

Acknowledgment

Long Story Short could never have come into print if it were not for the friends, family, and loves who became insightful creations for writing about and becoming part of my time, my place, and myself.

Written observations have been woven into poetry and stories throughout my life. As such, there are those who may not recognize themselves within the framework presented, but they are very, very real.

I am grateful for the support and energy supplied by Anna S., who pushed, propelled, prodded, and dragged me kicking and screaming while walking this journey with me. Without her confidence in me and constant friendship, I could not have pulled myself up by my bootstraps to tackle what seemed an impossible goal and reach the dream of becoming a published author.

My gratitude and humility is immense in completing the task at hand and giving readers, hopefully, words and images to relate to by seeing something of themselves or others through my eyes and writings.

Poetic License
(*Licentia Poetica*)

To do good things
in the world,
first you must know
who you are and
what gives meaning
to your **life**.
—Robert Browning

Karma

Walks with purpose and intention by her side
Determined, resolute, unflinching
She ties back her hair away from sightless eyes
She is the bearer of consequence
She carries no pity or regret with her
Only another's destiny set in motion by their actions
Unknowing, uncaring, unremorseful

Karma doesn't need to weigh the right or wrong
Shoulders back, head held high, focused on fate's calling
She simply carries herself with intention and grace
She can travel as slow or as fast as the journey takes
For she is time-honored and timeworn
Distance and destination guide her
Time waits for her only

Truth Is a Slippery Slope

What is the truth?
>Is it my version?
>Is it your version?
>Is it a concept that develops with time or with you?

Are you able to hear the truth?
>Live with the truth
>Die with the truth
>Be careful how you answer

You could be setting yourself up for more than the truth
>Do you lead a daily life of truth or only when it suits you?
>Do you tell the truth when asked?
>Do you cloak the truth as a flimsy version?

Or do you rely on "it's the truth" even if it hurts someone?
>They say a lie is only allowed to save a friend
>But does truth do the same?
>Do you lean on truth to disarm someone, hurt someone, save yourself?

Is truth in the eye of the beholder or hidden in the heart of the giver?
>"Tell me a lie is" often kinder than
>"Tell me the truth"
>Tell me, tell me, tell me

Who are you to offer the truth when asked, let alone when you are not asked?
Truth is a slippery slope, indeed
Better to see truth with your own eyes and heart, keeping it to yourself

Memory

He told her he went to see a "memory" with another
A memory they had shared

Is he an idiot?
Doesn't he understand how it will make her feel?

Is she an idiot?
To go with him and listen to the memory of another

Am I an idiot?
To listen and think, what a sweet thing to tell me

We're all idiots
He for going with another
She for listening about another
And
Me for understanding

Fini

Look at Me

Stop playing with
Your iPhone
Your iPad
Your Blackberry
Your cell phone
Your whatever
OK—*stop* texting, then, please
Talk to me
Look at me
I'm here
I'm real
A person
I should be the important one to you
Not a text
Not an afterthought
Not a rock sitting across from you
In fact, never mind
Text away
Really
Go ahead
I don't care
It's fine
You really have nothing to say to me
Nor I to you
Play at your technology
And don't worry about your life and
What you are turning into—a driven machine, head down, thumbs ready
Incapable of sustaining a conversation, let alone a thought
Text
Text
Text
Away

Words Without Thought

Words without thought spill from the mouth
Often times
Their meaning is misinterpreted, misread, misunderstood

But
Thoughts coming from the heart
Flow with joy, sadness, exquisite memories
Perhaps from a sound, a smell, a voice, a visual
Better to hold a thought than a word
Better to feel than interpret
So please leave me with my thoughts

And
Not your words
I want to hold on to my thoughts
Because long after you forget what someone has said
You will always remember how they made you feel

Dancing with Madness

Wrapped up in arms unknown
Keeping movement with the music

Fast, slow, swaying to the rhythm
Trying to keep up with the steps

I love to dance
I am a good dancer

Why am I stumbling, tripping?
Why can't I keep up with the music?

Hold me closer, tighter, please
Hold me so I can follow your lead, *please*

The music is so loud, so harsh, so bright
Dazed and sick with the sight and sound

I am dancing with madness
I am dancing with myself

Elevator Chatter

Is there no policy
Or
Politically correct way
To
Behave in an elevator
Answer: Obviously, not
It is simple, however
Up
Down
Look forward
Step out
Step in
Pay attention
Stop talking on that phone
Know where you are
Know where you are going
Move
Move
Move
OMG
I'm going crazy

I Am Unable

I am unable to speak
from holding my tongue
biting my tongue
too many times

I am unable to move
from standing still
not knowing which way to turn
too many times

I am unable to see
from being blinded by light
closing my eyes to the truth
too many times

I am unable to hear
from words that assault
turning away from the sounds
too many times

I am unable to breathe
from the loss of freedom
holding on to myself
too many times

Somewhere in Between

The truth and the lie
Is
The memory
The heart
But
Whose memory
Whose heart
Holds the key?
Is it mine?
Is it yours?
Somewhere in Between
Such a distance
Such a long journey
No one is able to breathe in
Forgiveness
Love
Kindness
Only
Godly righteousness
Indignant betrayal
Holy arrogance

Somewhere in Between

The Givers
The Takers

My mom always said
"Child, there are givers and there are takers
It is up to you on who you want to be
Be careful because your life's destiny will be determined by your choice"

To give of yourself is selfless and depletes your financial resources
But
Immensely enriches your soul

To take for yourself is selfish and builds your financial resources
But
Your soul may be in danger of ruin

Which turn in the road?
Either way
Is fraught with decision and desires
You may be unable to prepare yourself for the consequences

But
You will surely know who you are and who you have become
By looking back

A Woman of Subtle Distinction

She possesses
an inner nature
of intrinsic reality
A true being
A life force of
heart and soul
Her essence is
delectable
succulent
interesting
fluid
discriminating
remarkable
elegant
regal
passionate
She carries with her
a spirit of substance
a center to life
inherited and treasured
commanding her own destiny
with bravery and nobility
Hers alone

Miss Manners

Please
Set the table,
Fork, knife, and spoon.

Etiquette first
And last, of course,
Do not falter.

Splendid looking,
Most importantly,
Above all else.

Sit down right now.
Sit up, sit straight.
Enjoy, partake.

You're not hungry?
Too stressed to eat?
How come? What's wrong?

You are leaving?
Choking on what?
Ladylikeness!

Leave.
However, you're going to miss
The "just desserts."

Chanel, Gucci, Louis Vuitton, Juicy Couture, Burberry, Balenciaga

Walking down the street
She simply states
"I only buy purses with a name"
I start laughing, thinking
She is joking
She is not
She is serious

I stop and look at her
"Really? *Wow*, OK, then"
Are the only words I can spit out at her
She
Proceeds to just keep walking down the street
Unaware
Unknowing
Unconscious

Opportunist

She was small of stature
But
Large in presence
When she walked into a room
She entered as a force
When she walked out of a room
The air left with her

Hers was a world of noncompromise
A world of nonnegotiation
A world of remembrance
A slight was memorialized
A disagreement held dear
An error unforgivable

An earned reputation without loyalty
Sidled up to an air of infallibility
No one questioned who she was
Chasing only where she was

Black and Blue

Flowers always came
The day after he hit her
The tears always flowed with self-loathing
The day after he hit her
Promises, promises, promises
The day after he hit her
"Forgive me, I'll never do it again" rang out
The day after he hit her

But then, again, the anger would descend
Never knowing the why or when or where
Becoming conscious of a sound, a movement, a sign
In order to retreat, to run, to hide
No one to rescue her
No one to tell
Embarrassed, scared, alone, afraid, unheard
And then
Enough
Enough
She crawls out of the abyss
And
Into the light

Oreo

"The kids say you're white"
"They do?"
"Uh-huh"
"Well, honey, I am"
"Oh"
"You OK with that?"
"I guess"
"Want to talk about it?"
"Not really"
"When you do, you just let me know"
"Yeah, OK"
"Baby, I love you"
"I love you too, Mommy"

Love isn't love
until you share it
with others.
—Unknown

Could Have Been

Life interrupted by time and distance and differences
Talk used to be the lifeline to hold on to you

And now, it seems so disconnected and yet strangely familiar
Reconnection, but with a thirty-second-delay response

Not so bad—just sad to remember what was and now what is
But then, time, distance, and differences do that

Now and then, faintly bumping into each other
Loves and memories retained lose their significance and urgency

Creating a past of ethereal ghosts dancing wordlessly and effortlessly
Through a minefield of what "could have been"

Left Behind

You are left behind
And you don't understand why
Was it something you did?
Something you didn't do?
You try to make sense of the why
Without asking *why*
But of course, you can't
Because it wasn't you
It was never a matter of you
You didn't do anything wrong
It was him
And he doesn't even know the why
Stop putting yourself through hell
And live your life, not his
It is your time
Your heart will heal, and promises will be kept
But
Blessedly, by another

Late Sunday Afternoon

Late Sunday afternoon

When the day comes to an end

And the evening reaches up to pull the setting sun to her

Quietly with sound and movement standing still

Lazy and content on sheets of lost time

Knowing, but for a moment, all is well

Is when I miss him the most

To the Abyss

Extending your hand to lead me
to the dance floor
to your life
to my destiny
to my passion
to myself

And now

Extending my hand to lead you
to the kitchen
to the bathroom
to the bedroom
to the indignities
Of our life
Together

I

I am not alone
I am with you
I turned away
For just a moment

And

You were gone
Where did you go?
I am with you

Do you not remember?
I am with you
I am
I

Best Friends

Living, laughing, loving best friends
Completing one another, treasuring moments
Spent in each other's arms in a world within a world
Time away, one from the other, was always rare

He would look for her in a crowded room
She would catch his eye from across the floor
They were in each other's eyes and hearts
Never straying far from the sight and sound of each

And then, he left her alone with memories
No arms around one another to keep her warm
No eyes across a crowded room to catch the sight of him
Living, laughing, loving became only a memory
Of
Best friends

The Wife
Her Husband
His Mistress

The Wife

The restaurant was beautiful.
The view was spectacular.
The ambience was everything it should be.
And she knew why he brought her here.
They had been here together. He was lazy that way.
She looked at him from across the table as if he were a microorganism to be examined.
She leaned forward and said, "There are three things I cannot stand the taste of."
He lifted up his eyes from the menu and cocked his head as if wondering what she would say.
"Cilantro, scotch, and your cum."
"Well, my dear, you really won't have to worry about that this evening."

Her Husband

He just wanted to wake up next to the one person he was in love with.
And it wasn't his wife.
A life of excess and drama for the entire marriage had become unbearable.
But he stayed because he was a coward, and she knew he was.
He had to get drunk in order to survive her onslaught of words.
"Here's to the wound that never heals," he belligerently toasted.
Because that was who she was to him.
There would be no going back or forward.
There would just be this howling mimicry
of a life together that neither of them wanted.

His Mistress

She loved to relay this story:

"Three people are in a small boat on a lake when the weather turns unpredictably stormy.

The three people are the wife, her husband, and his mistress.

The wife and his mistress fall overboard.

The husband can only save one and is forced to make a decision on who to rescue.

He saves the wife.

Why?

Because

The mistress will understand."

And

She does.

She understands.

She

She arched, reaching up for him
clawing her way up his back, drowning in her greed
pulling him closer, tighter into this wave of heat.

She needed to quench her thirst and lust and saw
no reason or remorse in returning to insanity.
It did not matter where he had been or where he was going.

She was drunk with the craving and lusting for him, and
what mattered was the insatiable appetite he brought to her.
Sodden with the taste, smell, and feel of sodomy and perversion.

She was her master's obedient slut, whore, and she reveled in the words
he would spew as he came and charged inside, turning her
over and merciless impaling her lust as she pushed back into him.

This was not love.
This was madness.
This was obscene.
This was brilliant.

Unhinged

The angry sound of his words on paper rang in her head
as if it would really make a difference in her life.

He had no way of knowing that she was already dead inside.
She no longer could look or care about what she read
for she had ceased long ago to be his wife.

The angry sound of his words on paper rang in her head
as if it would really make a difference in her life.

But, God help her, it did.

god

You were a god to me
Did you know that?
Well, how could you?
You were too busy being a god
And I was too in awe to notice that you weren't

Mortals and gods don't mix well
In fact, gods don't mix at all
And so the story ends before its time
One of confusion, hurt, and disillusionment
But then I am merely a mortal

You wouldn't have known those emotions
Simply because you believe you are a god
And unworthy of such pedestrian feelings
god
How I hate that about you

When

When you are here
Or I am there

When time is never enough
Or time gives room

When life opens a door
Or shuts one

When you are lustful
Or can give your all

When your breath is on me
Or my mouth is in you

When you can give me
A great scotch
A great slow dance
A great long kiss

When

Achilles' Heel

She was his sense of wonder
His lover
His muse
His alone to touch
Hold tender
Amuse

'til Achilles' heel
Unfurled
With abuse

An Evening to Play at Seduction

Just time enough knowing
The player and the game

Savoring the taste and the sound
Trading words and breathing
Satisfying the craving and desire

Come to me as you will
I'll crawl from inside out
In a savage, satanic quest

Mind fucking until filled
With one's own wetness
Quelled for the moment

Until
Rising
Again

Emotional Affair

"Any time, any place"
The boy tells her
She laughs to herself
An inside joke only they understand

The two of them
Quiet as mice
Wordy as magpies
Together in thought and deed

Who are these two?
Does it really matter?
Simply, "tea for two"
And "two for tea"

Lone Ranger and Tonto
Batman and Robin
Mork and Mindy
Homer and Marge

A twosome
A duo
A pair

Six Feet Deep

She just stood there as an interested voyeur.
How relevant, no one knew or cared.
She was as Lot's wife.
Turning back, longing for the wickedness of pleasure once provided her.
She could not move until the thoughts of him were buried six feet deep.

And then, she simply, quietly turned around, walked away from her penance.
Cloaked in a shadow of indifference, shoulders upright, eyes straight ahead.
Accompanied only by resignation and resiliency.
It mattered not where she was going, for he was no longer her concern.

He had disfranchised her a very long time ago and began a new life of his own.
One he could start afresh, afire, alone.
But he had never loved her as she had him.
"Ciao, thank you, I'll be fine" tumbled softly from the once-coveted mouth.

Tears wouldn't come, for she had already dried up and blown away.
The entire relationship was summed up with the sardonic toast her lover would always
Give, "Here's to the wound that never heals."
She could not live without him, and now, seductively smiling, she had.

Dreaming

Always of you
Perplexing
Troubling

Removed you
From my mind
From my heart

But

There you are
Haunting me
Taunting me

I am forever
Lost to you
In my dreams

Taken

The sound of his voice
the feel of his touch
the breath on my back
and I am totally caught again.
Without reason, I throw away logic
and submit to an illusion of being
taken away again and again and again.

I am defeated in resisting or retreating.
Usher in the whips and chains and shackle
me against my will so I have no esteem left.
Make me ache and grieve for that which I cannot
control or release. Carry me away and down into the
depths of depravity, for that is where I long to lay and
submerge myself within your loins.

Begging for release, do not rescue me from myself, but
take me lower and deeper until I cannot breathe or hear or
see without you on top, behind, pulling me into myself.
Ransack and savage me till I am engorged with the mercy of
ignorance. For the sound of your voice, the feel of your touch
your breath on my back is all that matters to me until
I am deaf, dumb, blind to anyone or anything, but you.

Forgotten Memories

Every once in a while, I forget
I forget you
I forget me
I forget us

Purposely

Because remembering
Hurts my heart
Stops me from
Moving
Feeling
Lusting

And then
I go on
As if
We never were

So What

So you loved me for a while
But I loved you longer

So you betrayed all
While I kept the integrity intact

So you were charming and alluring
I was so head over heels in awe

So there never seemed to be time enough
And then the sand escaped the hourglass

So you left me far behind with regrets and memories
Stored so tightly away there was no escape

So there was a time that was so sweet
Only to turn over on its head with sorrow

So?
So what

The Green Dress

She appeared in a green dress
Nothing was said
Nothing need be

She simply knelt down in front of him
Unsnapping
Unbuttoning

She took him in her warmth
Held him
Swallowed him

She left the same way she came
Nothing was said
Nothing need be

He lay back, spent
A trick by his friends?
A trick of his imagination?

Who was she?
It really didn't matter
Damn

Reflect.
Recall.
Remember.
—Unknown

Kaleidoscope of Memories

We three loved the sound, smell, sight, and feel of the ocean
Creating and holding memories captive, warming and releasing
Playing hide-and-seek with the ocean
Beckoning fingers of surf and sound reach for me

He would always hum "Red Sails in the Sunset" to her
She would always laugh without pretense
They were a couple. I made us a family
I would always feel the love between them

They told me I could hear the ocean if I held the shell to my ear
I could because I believe in childlike things
The shell still carries the ocean's sound to me

And then, too soon
Grief with her tears carried different sounds
Sounds that he was no more
I kept myself inside myself so she wouldn't worry

Pushing toes of ten into the sand, releasing them to the sun
I look out to wet blue, and soft memories cut at me
A remembrance of a young family

A castle of sand built by a family never meant to
Outlast the precious gift of time
Sacrificed to outstretched hands that kept
Forever pulling away at the small grains of sand in the hourglass
A family now torn apart by the loss of a father

Eyes squinting up toward a blinding yellow heat
Playing with a kaleidoscope of memories
Turning warmth into contentment
Listening to the sounds of yesterday
A potpourri of life
I grew beyond his flower of youth

We three loved the sound, smell, sight, and feel of the ocean

I still do

Widowed

When I was small, she left me behind
No one spoke of where or why
Her name was spoken in hushed tones
As if we were in a church
As if she never existed
As if a terrible deed had been done

They said she needed rest, needed to leave us
But I could not understand why
Soulful eyes glanced away from questioning eyes
I was a quiet child, seldom bothersome, wise beyond years
Why would she need to leave me behind?

Burdens heavy to carry, widowed young
Leaving me with a grandmother who shared her Christian name with me
But not her love
A coldness a child was even unable to thaw
An insurmountable distanced of hurt

She came back to us changed, different from before
We were changed now too from her absence
We never lived happily ever after when she returned
She was trying to survive a loss
A loss that time could not heal
I asked her once, only once, when I became mother to my child
Why she left me behind
But she could never say why
She could never find an answer to the question in the old eyes of a young girl
And finally
I stopped asking or caring

Hardness of Heart

I promise to mourn you for a day or two
  Perhaps a week, but really, no more
  For you left us a very long time ago with
  No thought or care in your heart for a wife and young son

Why do you think I can go back to loving you now?
  Lapse in memory and blinded by your own glory
  Poor you, living a lie was easy and now alone
  So you are afraid of dying without a soul. So what?

Cry, I cannot for you, but only for the life you tossed aside
  Caps off to your self-indulgence, arrogance, and little else
  More I cannot say, except if it is forgiveness you are seeking
  Go to a higher power to lick your wounds, not I

Lie to others if you must, but not to yourself or me and mine
  Relapse if you are able to lash out at life's end with self-pity
  Exhausted from listening to your tale of woe now
  Foe you are not, but a very close second

Me and My Pop

He was my hero, my pop
He, I could always depend upon
Anything I needed or wanted
He provided

And now

I am lost without him
He no longer is
He is here, but not "here"
And I have to become the parent to him

Does that make me "the hero"?
Am I to be depended upon
Anything he needs or wants?
How do I do that?

I don't think I'm ready to change roles
I'm still a kid
Who needs her pop

Child of Mine

My child
Fast to grow up
Quick to wound
Fast to bleed me
Without thought of
Or
Consequence
She leaves

A Mother's Love

Your voice of anger is palpable
The pain of a knife cutting through my heart
Words spill as raw sewage from your mouth
I am not able or willing to listen or look at you

For when you are like this
I do not have enough hands to cover
My eyes, my ears, my mouth, my heart
You are not my son; you have become my enemy

You are not the child I once held
You are now the one I push away
Confusion and chaos reign without limit
Within your brilliant mind and harsh words

I can only stand with my bleeding heart in hand
I am unable to comfort or calm or staunch the blood
You are unable to be my son
I am unable to be your mother

The One

The one who was wanted most
Never wanted anyone

The one who was loved best
Loved back the least

The one who laughed the loudest
Always cried the softest

The one who was given gifts of love
Took without giving in return

The one who was found
Is now the one who is lost

The one who needed what I could not give
Simply turned and walked away

Beautiful Boy

My firstborn son inhabited my world completely with fascination and wonder
> It would be a lifetime of some fourteen years before a sibling came
> along
> Prior to that time, we were a team, a duo—unbroken without
> thoughts of betrayal or hurt
> Coming toward us without hesitation

I wanted to create a family for us, a home—little did I know, we were already
a family, a home
> For what came into our life was an illusion, an inquisition, a deluded
> belief in someone
> We were rescued, but of course, there are times the rescuer is not
> the protector you
> Thought but a lure to entice and capture those who refuse to
> relinquish

Words screamed in my head
> "Be careful of the man who does not like himself, for you are his next
> victim"
> Looking back is painful
> But looking forward at that time was an unforgiving landscape of
> fear, recrimination
> For acts we didn't even know we had committed

Waiting for an opportunity to escape, shuttling this beautiful child away from
me to protect him
> Proceeding to make misstep after misstep—both of creating chaos,
> carrying the

Burden of the past into the unknown future was like walking on eggshells blindfolded
Losing face, losing ground, losing heart, losing one's heart and mind

Running away from the destruction was the only course of action
And we have been running ever since
My beautiful boy and I

Sons

One is his
One is another's

One sits on his lap
One sits across the room

One is perfect
One will never be

One reaches up to touch him
One can never reach that far

One is loved
One is loved
One is loved

Lost and Found

I have a firstborn son who has left our home
A home he no longer wants to call his own.
He is being held in Lost and Found, waiting for someone to claim him.
He is a woeful child, too young to be on his own, too old for me to hold.

He shuns commitment—a fledgling having left too soon.
I want to run after him, but he will not be caught.
He is running too fast and is unable to look back.
He is away from me, carrying his anger and pain alone.

Is he really the son I wanted or some waif drifting outside my door?
Have I gone too far or not far enough?
Am I to suffer for him or allow his pain to strengthen him?

How will I know when my job is finished?
And if it was a job well done, will you be the judge and jury?
My experience is a method of trial and error.
I wear guilt as a shawl around my shoulders.

I am a mother of doubt and fear, bearing silent prayers
For his hopeful tomorrow
And lost yesterday
Waiting for him to be found.

Delinquent

He is a juvenile delinquent.

This is why his grandmother and I are sitting in a courtroom.

We look around nervously for the sight of him.

But all we see are other mothers looking around for the sight of their delinquents.

No fathers appear to be part of this exclusive club. But then, no one really expects them to be.

And absolutely, we are all scared out of our minds with anger, worry, and an overwhelming scent of sadness that invades the walls, the benches, and the air surrounding us, so breathing is difficult and held before making a strangling sound when one tries to speak.

I bend my head down, if just to try and compose myself when I hear my mother moan words, saying, "Oh god, there he is."

I hear the shuffling of leg restraints first and look up as we both watch him shuffling in with handcuffs and restraints without understanding that, of course, the court is afraid they will run to where God only knows.

He keeps his head down with his eyes averted.

He appears to be bluffing his way through this, acting defiantly, unaffected by his surroundings.

And my lovely, sweet mom tries to catch his eye to offer a small wave to him as if he is onstage, waiting to be acknowledged.

We three are in this melodrama together whether or not we want to be. Here we are.

The sitting judge is impervious to his party of delinquents. One can sense his overwhelming fatigue at attempting to determine who is worth saving and wasted words spoken to the faceless youths who cannot or will not listen. And the mothers and grandmothers are simply present, waiting just to rescue their young—the ones they carried in their wombs and arms and hearts.

When we are approached by the appointed defender of youth, we follow him as if we are blinded by shame and remorse. We know it is our fault because the looks of and from the court scream to us, *It is your fault.* And of course, they are right. It must be our fault. Our eyes are sore and red from crying, our shoulders are bent with worry, and our hearts have been broken. My mom and I hold on to each other. Our pockets feel as if they are filled with stones so we can hardly make one foot step in front of the other.

We sit down at a steel table in steel chairs across from our delinquent and his court-appointed attorney.

We try to will him to raise his head so we can find him in his eyes.

But he is unable or unwilling to accommodate these motherly wishes.

We talk only about the deed that took him from our protection and placed him in the middle of hell.

We talk about the how, the what, and the why of his stupidity and how it landed him here.

We talk about how to get him out and back with us. While at least with his grandmother as his guardian as I am tethered right now to his stepfather, who wants nothing to do with the situation as he claims, "Not my son, not my problem."

Perfect.

And all I want to do is lay myself down for a thousand years and then wake up blissfully happy and secure.

But of course, that is not to be.

There is work to be done and fences to be mended—hearts that are bleeding.

An unknown world before us that is careening out of control in so many ways.

We are now brought before the judge to plead our delinquent's case.

His indifference is blistering.

My mom's hearing aid is squealing at a high pitch as if on trial itself.

And I hold her hand to calm her and myself.

"Goddamn hearing aid," she softly says to herself and begins talking to the judge about this delinquent she loves and will watch over. He need not worry that they will return to his court.

She will make sure of that. He is a good boy.

Oh god, the judge has heard these same words over again throughout his years on this bench.

But he listens. Maybe it was her hearing aid that opened his heart.

After offering my mom a somewhat benevolent face, the judge turns to the delinquent and rolls into him with his words, his admonitions, his warning about facing him again, and about how his mom and my mom have been there for him and how he could do this to them.

Ad nauseam with his words, finally the judge asks the delinquent to stand for sentencing and hands him over to my mom with probation.

The delinquent is trying to hold back the tears and bravely trying not to fall on his knees with sheer gratitude.

We leave the courtroom together, blinded by the outside light.

All three of us are in a kind of group hug/walk thing, afraid to let go of each other.

No words are spoken. No words need be.

We drive away with our thoughts recklessly strung together by another chance given that we will be able to make this better for the delinquent.

And then, softly the tears flow from three sets of eyes—the one driving, the one looking out the window, and the one reaching back to hold the delinquent's unsure hand.

The Family

My heart is breaking with grief.

As much for the loss of a loved family member as for the loss of never knowing me and mine.

But because of judgments made long ago at another time, my children grew up without my family.

I was prepared to go it alone. And I did—too many times for too many reasons.

My children never knew the hurt and pain of being dismissed as a family member, and they never knew the history.

I did.

I do.

But now, with a death staring at us, they stand here beside me, wondering without questioning as to who this family is and why we weren't part of it—not in life, not even in death.

Such a loss for all of us.

But you stand tall, straighten your attitude up, forgive, and carry on in spite or because of.

I only know the grief is never ending because the hurt and pain is so deeply hidden that you are blinded by the knowledge that there was absolutely nothing you did wrong or could have done to change the outcome of your own family's feelings toward you and yours.

A betrayal to them of insurmountable heights that is dizzying to even comprehend or understand.

Do they miss us?

They don't even know us!

Believe

If I were to tell you
You are not alone
Would you believe me?
If I were to whisper
You will always have someone who cares
Would you believe me?
If I were to sing a song to remind you of who you are
Would you not believe me?
If I were to write poetry to memorialize you
Wouldn't you believe me?
If I were to write in the sky who you are and why
Would you not look up and know it was you?
If all who love you
Do
Just
Believe in them
Believe in me
Believe in you

Tell me a fact
and
I will listen.

Tell me the truth
and
I will believe.

Tell me a story
and
It will live in my heart forever.
—Unknown